AN INSIDE JOB™

SIMPLE & EFFECTIVE SELF-HYPNOSIS
FOR TRANSFORMATIONAL CHANGE

Tricia Woolfrey and Helen Craven

First published in Great Britain in 2012 by
Verity Publishing

British Library Cataloguing in Publication Data
A CIP catalogue record for this book is available from
the British Library

ISBN 978-0-9558374-6-3

Cover Photo: ©fotolia

Printed in Great Britain by
Printed in Great Britain by Shore Books and Design
Blackborough End, Norfolk PE32 1SF

DISCLAIMER

Although the authors have made every effort to ensure the accuracy and completeness of information contained in this book, no responsibility is assumed for errors, inaccuracies, omissions or inconsistencies herein. Any slights of people, places or organisations are unintentional.

The contents of this book are intended to provide general information only and do not attempt to give advice relating to specific circumstances.

The efficacy of the system is in direct proportion to the commitment of the reader to the end result. Persistence and diligence are required.

Anyone suffering from personality disorders or severe emotional problems should first seek the help of a competent therapist.

Dedicated to the memory of Lynda Dawn Baxter,
whose life inspired a journey into hypnosis.

With thanks to all those who helped and supported
us in the creation of this book:

Jill Anderson

John McBurnie

Claudine Bruce

Will Bruce

Geraldine Cawthorne

Augustus John Craven

Stephen Harold

Nicky Rudd

Linda Sluys

Foszia Turner Stylianou

CONTENTS

I

WE MIND, YOU MATTER
AN INTRODUCTION

The idea for this book came about when the authors attended a seminar together. Having known each other for some years and having developed a professional respect for each other's work as well as a warm friendship, they decided to work jointly on a project to put the basic practices they regularly use with clients into an easy-to-follow book form. This is intended to serve three types of interested reader who would like to benefit from the empowerment of self-hypnosis:

1. Those who, for whatever reason, don't want to embark on one-to-one therapy sessions;

2. Those who would like to enhance the personal development and stress management work they are already doing;

3. Those who are already experiencing hypnosis work with a therapist, but who would like written reminders of exercises they can practice on their own, together with a little more background information.

Too often we rely on everything **outside** of us to make everything OK **inside** of us. Believing that to be happy, we need the right job; the right house; the right labels on our clothes; the right car in our sweeping driveway; our partner to say and do the right things; our children to be appreciative; etc. You might call it "if-only living", but it is an illusion because it's transient and conditional. Happiness, success and confidence are An Inside Job™. You **can** be happy even if you aren't doing quite the job you dreamed of; if your clothes are from the High Street instead of designer label; if your car is care-worn and parked on the roadside instead of in the drive of your dream home; and even if your partner doesn't appreciate you in the way you think they should. When you sort yourself out from the inside, the things on the outside matter less. You become more of who you are, more peaceful, less stressed, more inspired, less bothered by the small irritations, more appreciative of the little things such as a smile on a small child's face; the happy wagging tail of a dog; the first daffodil of spring.

When we feel positive on the inside we start to impact the outside world and, at the same time, attract more positivity and success into our lives. What we focus on we attract. You will notice that we repeat this throughout the book. We do this deliberately, because it is such an important point to remember.

We often hear of people saying that it takes a huge life event, such as cancer, to make us appreciate what we have and who we are. But you can do that now, by taking charge and looking at things differently. Self-hypnosis can help you to do that more simply and effectively than many other techniques - and it all happens within the privacy of your own mind.

The benefits of An Inside Job™ Self-Hypnosis practice are:

- A greater sense of peace and calm
- Emotional resilience so that you bounce back from setbacks more easily
- Increased motivation for life in general and your goals in particular
- Improved self-esteem
- The ability to see things positively
- See problems and errors as a chance to learn and grow
- Emotional healing
- Positive change whilst neutralising any resistance to change
- Resolution of inner conflict
- Greater self-awareness
- More patience
- Greater physical wellbeing [1]

The benefits will vary according to how you use it and how often you practice, but you can achieve all the above by targeting your self-hypnosis practice appropriately. You will learn how to do this in the chapters which follow.

---

[1] In Molecules of Emotion, Candace B Pert, PhD talks about how our emotions and their biological components establish the crucial link between mind and body, and how our feelings affect both our health and well-being.

Self-Hypnosis CD

We have included a CD to assist your self-hypnosis practice. It will guide you through each of the stages and includes a "double-induction" (where you will hear two voices) which creates a more powerful hypnotic experience. The use of our voices and the choice of our words are designed to increase your depth of trance to alpha or theta (see Chapter 3). If possible, listen to the CD on your headphones to maximise the impact.

The CD is intended for you to actively engage with it by bringing in your own suggestions and visualisations (see Chapters 5 and 6).

It also gives you the opportunity to experience the 4th level where you will deal with inner conflict (see Chapter 7) should you choose.

In the meantime, the authors, Tricia Woolfrey and Helen Craven, share with you their personal stories:

Tricia's Story

My first experience of hypnotherapy occurred when I was 18. I had had a phobia of cats since the age of 5. We had a family cat which I adored but it attacked me and then ran away. It never came back. Since that day, I started to shy away from any cats I encountered, expecting to be attacked again. Over a fairly short space of time, this became a phobia which would plague me for years to come. It had caused me many problems, huge embarrassment and was limiting me socially.

A phobia is an irrational fear. I knew that my fear was ridiculous and that there was no real danger. Indeed, some people can develop a fear of standing up, or buttons, and other seemingly innocuous things. I don't recall sustaining any actual injury, yet the feeling was very real and debilitating. I would have preferred to have driven a knife through my heart than face my fear.

I was desperate and saw a psychologist from the NHS who kindly told me that the phobia was because my family didn't love me, and nor did my future husband, to whom I have now been married for 26 years. Even worse, she also told me that the only way to conquer the fear was to sit with a cat. Well **that** wasn't going to happen!

So I decided to try a kinder route and looked into hypnotherapy. I didn't quite know what to expect but somehow expected something different (this is a very common experience in people who undergo hypnotherapy).

It took a couple of sessions with different hypnotherapists before I settled on one who was very warm and pleasant. I was, at the time, terribly shy and self-conscious. At no time did I feel relaxed. I was completely aware of everything he said. I felt a "performance pressure" to be a good subject and so very consciously followed his instructions, while thinking to myself that it "wasn't working".

Nevertheless, I booked for several sessions because I was so desperate. Each time was the same. I didn't feel "under". No relaxation. Completely aware of everything, including my intrusive thoughts. Yet this lovely gentleman cured me – I had a cat on my lap for the first time in 13 years. In fact it was the first time I was in the same room as a cat.

To be honest, the fear returned after some time but to a much lesser extent. I hadn't realised the importance of continuing the treatment beyond the initial breakthrough – very important for long-term results. By stopping too soon (as soon as I had the cat on my lap), we failed to tackle the underlying cause of the fear. We simply reduced the symptom of the fear and left me open to it recurring under similar circumstances in the future. That was a good learning for me in later years.

Another reason that the fear came back was because for 13 years it had been my habit to avoid the situation. After the hypnotherapy, again through habit, I continued to avoid cats. This built the fear back up again, though never as strongly as it was previously.

And I always addressed the issue with a quick fix which, again, did not deal with the root cause. Now, I am 95% free. Most people don't know of my problem. Not facing fears by continually avoiding them is one way – probably the most common – in which phobias build.

I had no idea then that in years to come I would become a hypnotherapist myself. I came to it through an NLP (Neuro Linguistic Programming) course which I did whilst working as a Human Resources Director. In this 18 month course, we were taught hypnotic language. This was the introduction which whetted my appetite for the real thing. I enrolled on a hypnotherapy/psychotherapy course and here I am, having been a hypnotherapist for 14 years at the time of writing and absolutely loving it. Helping people resolve their issues is a very fulfilling career.

I have witnessed the transformation of many, many lives as I have worked with clients on issues as diverse as self-esteem, anxiety, anger management, weight loss, interview preparation, assertiveness and building positive relationships.

Whilst some experience hypnotherapy as a magic bullet, results are more often cumulative. Yet others will feel worse before they feel better, though this is rare. The important thing is that it is a **process**. It is a **partnership** which requires your willing co-operation, rather than something which is done **to** you. And quite rightly – a good therapist will put you in control of your life and empower you.

Helen's Story

It began back in 1997 when I was setting up a complementary health clinic with a multi-disciplinary approach. I had always thought of hypnosis as a bit of quackery. I was a sceptic who hadn't even thought of hypnotherapy as a part of the clinic set-up. I liked being in control and wasn't open to someone else taking over my thought processes - thank you very much! But then, I didn't know anything much about it.

Having been approached separately by two very professional and very interesting hypnotherapists who wanted to work in the clinic, I thought I should open my mind and at least find out something about it. One Friday evening I had a 'sample' session to see how the person worked and to experience the 'trance state'. I had experienced umpteen other therapies, as well as practicing yoga and meditation for years, but this took me to a state of relaxation that was deeper than anything I'd experienced before. I didn't want to come back to my conscious awareness as it was so good to float in my inner world. I was hooked.

The following morning I was in a crowded supermarket and found myself in a calm state, smiling at screaming toddlers, being polite to everyone who pushed passed me and generally being extremely chilled out. I literally pinched myself. This was so alien compared to how I usually felt having to shop on a Saturday morning. Then I remembered 'that darned hypnotherapist'! I remembered a suggestion about a feel-good capsule that would slow release for the next few days - and it certainly did.

As the months went by I learned more and experienced more and that process continues to this day.

The real motivation for going into professional practice came when I worked with my sister. With the guidance and help of experienced hypnotherapists, I worked with my beloved sister when she was diagnosed with terminal cancer. She was always a positive and dynamic person, but when she was told that her cancer treatments hadn't worked and the tumours were advancing rapidly, it was as if she lost her very essence. In this mentally depleted state she agreed to work with me.

In one session the hypnosis techniques enabled her to find her inner strength. She lived for another two years despite medical expectation of a few months at the most. We continued to work together with hypnosis and although it didn't reverse the medical condition, she found a power within her that overcame pain and depression.

She was undergoing chemotherapy that felt like a searing, burning sensation which she dreaded. After her hypnotherapy sessions, she could relax through the chemotherapy, listening to a hypnosis CD and feeling fine. She enjoyed many special moments in those last two years and passed over very peacefully.

From that time, back in the late 1990's, I knew I had to share these techniques. I believe that if we all know how to work with our subconscious, to find peace and power, then the world will be a better place.

I consider that teaching self-hypnosis to my clients is an essential part of my therapy work and welcome the chance to spread this gift to a wider public.

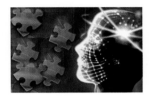

What is Hypnosis?

Hypnosis is a particular state of awareness where you are not fully awake but not asleep. You may feel relaxed or you may not. It is not the same as relaxation, though most people do relax, especially in self-hypnosis. You may recall that in Tricia's hypnotherapy treatment at the age of 18, she didn't feel relaxed, yet she was still hypnotised and the therapy worked for her.

People expect to be transported to a "third dimension" but it is actually a perfectly natural state which we all enter into every day of our lives. A good example is if you are engrossed in a film, or you are driving to work and find that you have arrived without any recollection of the journey.

Some people feel tingly, or numb, or heavy or light, or all of them, or none of them. Some people feel as though they have their eyes closed and nothing more than that.

Everybody is different. The biggest mistake anybody makes is to **try** to relax. Hypnosis is not a state of trying, rather a state of **allowing**. However you experience it is the right way for you to experience it. It is simply more enjoyable to relax.

Whilst a stage show suggests that hypnosis offers miraculous change, the stage hypnotist is not dealing with deep emotional issues. Rather they are using the state of hypnosis for entertainment. The volunteers know what they are agreeing to and want to be part of the entertainment process. There is no emotional agenda involved – just fun.

With hypnotherapy, by contrast, the natural state of hypnosis is used to deal with issues which may have existed for many years. Often the therapist has to work through layers of problems to get to the root and also through layers of self-awareness, vulnerability and denial. This is why it is important to work with an expert therapist if your issues are significant.

Hypnosis used for therapeutic benefit will consists of several parts:

1. **Induction**
   This is the doorway to the hypnotic state.

2. **Deepening**
   This deepens the hypnotic state to prepare the mind for suggestions or other therapeutic work.

3. Therapy

This can be in the form of :

Suggestion, which is the simplest form of therapy and will be explored in Chapter 5;

Regression, which involves taking the client back in time to deal with the root cause of the problem (we will not deal with this in this book as it must always be done with a qualified therapist who can work one-to-one with you);

Parts Therapy which resolves internal conflict (a form of which we will take you through in Chapter 7);

Metaphor and Language Patterns. These will be outside the remit of this book as they require a deeper level of knowledge which would require a book on its own. They are, however, incorporated into the CD.

4. Emerging

This brings the subject out of hypnosis and back into the here and now.

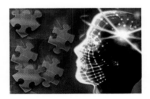

What is Self-Hypnosis?

Self-hypnosis is intentionally guiding yourself into the hypnotic state for self-improvement, stress management, emotional and spiritual hygiene.

Emotional hygiene is the ability to deal with any negative emotions as they arise rather than suppressing or repressing them. This enables us to:

- Respond appropriately and in proportion to the situation

- Let go of the need to control **everything** in life

- Take responsibility for those things that we can control

- Not worry ourselves over things which we are unable to impact

Spiritual hygiene can be described as:

- Removing any blocks to an inner feeling of peace, love and harmony

- The ability to deal more effectively with life's challenges

We don't want to get to the point where nothing will ever bother us ever again – that wouldn't be natural. Like living in the land of Stepford[2]. We want to **feel** our feelings to fully experience ourselves and our lives. What we want to achieve is:

---

[2]   This refers to the film The Stepford Wives where a young mother suspects that the frighteningly submissive housewives in her new idyllic neighbourhood may be robots created by their husbands.

- The ability to bounce back from setbacks more quickly

- The ability to trouble-shoot problems more effectively

- A greater sense of your self and your abilities

- A greater feeling of inner peace and resourcefulness

But, like an exercise bike that you buy to lose weight or get fit, it is only effective to the extent to which you use it. Daily practice will yield powerful results which will give you a significant return on the investment of your time.

We are happy to take our cars for a regular service, knowing that without it, they might break down. Self-hypnosis is like the maintenance and fine-tuning done by the mechanic, to ensure that it continues to run smoothly, and reliably take you where you want to go. Think of this as self maintenance - filling your tank with the fuel your mind, body and spirit need to help you meet the demands placed on you in your daily life.

In using the state of hypnosis for your own benefit, it too will be a process. You will be working through layers of the problem you want to deal with and results will be varied. Some people may notice results quickly, others may take longer. And yet others will not notice the changes until someone else points out how much more relaxed they are (this is very common!) Some people will feel incremental change and yet others may feel worse before they feel better (usually a sign of getting to the root so persistence is really important). Some people may also experience physical symptoms such as a sore throat, or tummy upsets. This is a sign that the mind-body is working things through.

The important thing is that you are taking charge of your life and this book will help you.

Important Note

If you have any deep-seated issues it may be appropriate to seek the help of a professional before starting to embark on your own journey of self-hypnosis. This is because sometimes, uncovering a painful past can cause emotional reactions that a professional can help you to deal with in ways which can be too challenging when working alone.

Additionally, in the unlikely event that this process should uncover deep-seated issues you were previously unaware of, then it is advisable to consult with a qualified professional.

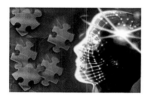

How this book is structured

We have already given you some background about hypnotherapy, what it is, and what it isn't. We will then give you details of the history of hypnotherapy – it has been around for a surprisingly long time! This will help you to understand the background and some of its credentials.

Then we will move into the more technical area where we describe the concept of the mind and the role that plays in the process of change and hypnosis.

Then, because there are a number of ways you can engage with this system, we have split it into four levels:

Level 1   Induction and Deepening

Takes you into self-hypnosis and helps you to relax your mind and body and to prepare you for the next stage. You will need this level for all other levels and it can be used on its own for a quick way to switch off and relax.

Level 2   Suggestions

This helps you to build on the foundations with goal setting and scripting powerful suggestions (affirmations) to enable you to create that change. Repetition is absolutely key in this phase, so invest your time. We have incorporated into your suggestions your natural responses. This has the effect of neutralising any resistance to change. The more you repeat the suggestion, the weaker your negative response will become.

Level 3   Visualisation

This chapter will show you how to visualise your goal as a powerful way of training your mind to achieve it. Some exceptional results can be achieved through the power of visualisation alone.

Level 4   Dealing with Inner Conflict

This enables you to deal with any blocks you have to creating positive change and specifically around internal conflict – where there is a part of you that wants change and a part of you that resists. This is an advanced form of self-hypnosis and is extremely powerful.

The authors have written this book together. However, out of necessity, parts have been written alone so may refer to the "I" of the initial author. It is difficult to write all of it without making such references. We do hope that this will not interfere with your enjoyment of the book and rest assured that both authors have collaborated fully to bring you the best in terms of advice and support.

When not referring to a particular individual, we will use the terms "him", "his" or "he" simply because they read more easily than "him/her", "his/her" and "he/she". Again, we do hope it doesn't interfere with your enjoyment of the book.

We are passionate about our work and about being able to help people take control of their lives. We believe that everyone deserves to be happy, healthy and fulfilled. We have written this book to help you reveal what's already there but is as yet undiscovered, so that you can live an authentic and fulfilling life.

Do remember to use the CD to make your self-hypnosis practice even more powerful.

Both of us regularly use self-hypnosis to help us in our daily lives. We sincerely hope that you gain as much benefit from it as we do.

Enjoy!

Helen Craven and Tricia Woolfrey

> *If you don't have a vision of the future,*
> *your future is threatened to be a*
> *repetition of the past.*
>
> **A R Bernard**

2

IN THE BEGINNING
THE HISTORY OF HYPNOSIS

In this chapter, we are going to look at why and how hypnosis and hypnotherapy began.

I'm sure all of us, at some time or another, have tried to make sense of our minds and how they work. Where do our thoughts come from and what exactly are "thoughts"?

Helen remembers as a small child pondering on what happened to her thoughts after she had thought them. Our bodies can be seen and scientifically explained. If we cut ourselves, we bleed and then the skin heals. We see it, we study it through dissection and microscopes, but our minds are still far from being fully understood by scientists. Like the air around us, the mind is invisible.

From the earliest times in recorded history there have been indications that hypnosis has been recognised and utilised.

The name **Hypnosis** was only coined in 1842 by the Scottish surgeon James Braid (see below), from the Greek **Hypnos**, which means "sleep". But the use of trance-states and sleep-states for healing and diagnosis is evident in many ancient and traditional civilisations. We now define a difference between

sleep and **hypnosis trance,** but there is a fine line between the two. We will explore this more in Chapter 3.

Egyptian Sleep Temples

Over 4000 years ago, the Egyptians had Sleep Temples dedicated to healing and invoking dreams in order to determine the appropriate treatment. They induced trance-states as one of the techniques to induce lucid dreaming, or dreams to inform the healing process.

Such temples also existed in the Middle East and Ancient Greece.

Sir Mortimer Wheeler unearthed a Roman Sleep Temple at Lydney Park, Gloucestershire in 1928, with the assistance of a young J R R Tolkien. This seems very apt for a man with such a creative imagination, as we now know that the subconscious mind feeds us both dreams and creativity. Maybe Golum would have been freed from his obsession with The Ring if he'd been treated in a Sleep Temple!

There is, at the time of writing, a Greek hypnotherapist working in Corfu, who has researched incubation or sleep temples and is using an adapted form of sleep temple therapy with powerful results.

The subjects in ancient Greek times would probably have been people for whom other therapies, such as herbal remedies, hadn't worked. They didn't just enter the sleep temples, they would have spent some time being prepared for the experience. They had to fast on particular foods and drink plenty of water to purify their bodies. They also had to attend a theatrical performance beforehand. Today we might link this to psychodrama work – it would have been a method to help them to link with, and identify, their own emotions.

They also had to walk down a long, dark corridor which was filled with non-poisonous snakes, in order to reach the temple. Apart from a possible fear-factor, the snake was a powerful symbol for healing and regeneration. We still see the snake on the Caduceus symbol used by medical academies and pharmacies. Today, imagining walking down a long, dark tunnel is sometimes used as an induction for regression work (where the hypnotherapist takes the subject back in time), so it would have helped induce a trance-state.

The patients would lay in hollows within the temple floor in a totally darkened room. They would hear incantations and be brushed with herbs and leaves – like laurel – which induce a mild hallucinogenic effect and then left to sleep and dream.

On awakening, the dreams would be acknowledged as a guide to the treatment required. As we now know, in deep trance our subconscious minds will reveal all kinds of memories and insights, from which we can learn, and once acknowledged, we can move on with a better understanding of ourselves.

Hippocrates and Aristotle

Hippocrates (460 BC – 370 BC) and Aristotle (384 BC-322 BC), in Ancient Greece, were amongst the first to write down their findings about medicine and healing. They wrote about the mind/body connection with regard to health, well-being and healing and particularly talked about the benefits of *deep relaxation* with regard to childbirth. Hypnosis is currently growing in popularity as a tool for enabling easier birthing, reducing or eliminating the need for medical interventions or pain control.

Hippocrates, even today, has a strong influence on the medical profession. The Hippocratic Oath is undertaken by doctors as part of their code of ethics, for example.

Mesmerism

Anton Mesmer (1734-1815), from a Swiss-German family, is considered the father of modern hypnosis, although his techniques might seem far removed from the contemporary hypnotherapist, his showmanship and his methods of sweeping his hands around the subjects body (sometimes for hours), might well have induced a trance-state.

He believed that a 'quasi magnetic fluid' was breathed in through the air and flowed through our blood and nervous system. If blocks were created in this flow, they manifested in physical and emotional problems. He initially used magnets to free the flow and then passed his hands around the body.

He achieved great success. The power of his suggestions, and the induction of the trance-state in the client, are the same principles by which we work today. However, the jealousy of his fellow doctors at his success, coupled with his pride and desire for fame, unfortunately led to his fall from favour.

It is acknowledged that he was a brilliant man, but his love of showmanship did give rise to the characterisation of the evil 'Svengali' figure with staring eyes and a magician's cloak, trying to control his unsuspecting 'victim'.

On reflection, if we recognise the principles of Traditional Chinese Medicine that informs such practices as acupuncture, shiatsu and reflexology, then Mesmer's theories of blocked energy flows around the body having a negative effect were well-founded.

John Elliotson

There were doctors in Britain who were interested in Mesmer's work. John Elliotson (1791-1868), a professor at London University, was keen to promote the principles, but it didn't find favour with his colleagues and he was forced to resign. However, he continued to spread the word and there was continued interest and published works on the subject.

James Braid

James Braid (1795-1860), an eye surgeon, advanced the process by discovering that if a person focused on a fixed object (the classic 'swinging watch' becoming the popular tool of the time), then a suggestible 'trance-state' could be induced much faster than the hand passes used in the Mesmeric process. He continued to explore what he now called 'hypnosis' and wrote an influential book on the subject: Neurypnology, or The Rationale of Nervous Sleep (1843).

James Esdaile

Possibly the most impressive proponent of hypnosis, by practical success rather than as a teacher, was James Esdaile (1808-1859). As a British surgeon working in India, he assisted in 300 major operations and over 1000 minor ones, using hypnosis as his only form of anaesthesia.

He had few resources and although chemical anaesthetics were being pioneered in Britain, they didn't reach his Indian outposts. His results were outstanding. Other surgeons in India at the time experienced an average mortality rate of 50%, whereas Esdaile's was only 5%.

He recognised hypnosis as a powerful tool for pain relief, but on his return to England the medical profession preferred to ignore his experience and promote their scientific advances with chemical pain relief. There was fame and financial gain to be had from these scientific advances, so hypnosis, yet again, was played down and dismissed.

Sigmund Freud

The father of psychoanalysis, who became a household name, Freud (1856-1939) was trained in hypnosis techniques. He initially used it extensively, but eventually abandoned the practice. It has been commonly accepted that he wasn't very good at it, so developed what came to be known as psychoanalysis as a new way of working.

However, it's interesting to note that he had his patients lying on a couch and sat where they couldn't see him, they could only hear his voice. This is not dissimilar to the hypnotherapist who has the client close their eyes and uses the voice to elicit the trance state to enable information to come through from the subconscious or to impart positive and healing suggestions.

Freud's influence may have diminished the growth and popularity of hypnosis, but there were always those who recognised it's potential.

Milton Erickson

Perhaps America led the way in the 20th Century, as far as cutting-edge developments in hypnosis were concerned. A book called 'Hypnosis and Suggestibility" by Clark Hull was published in the 1930's which re-kindled interest. However, most practitioners would recognise that the most significant person to really advance the practice of Hypnotherapy in the 20th Century has to be Milton H Erickson MD (1901-1980).

Milton Erickson had amazing perception. As a teenager he was stricken with polio, and he used self-hypnosis to deal with the severe pain he suffered. His condition forced him to observe, rather than take part in life. He therefore learned a great deal about human behaviour. More than that, he had the brilliance to find innovative ways to communicate with others and trigger healing through that communication. His techniques are taught and used with great effect to this day. He cleverly turned metaphor, humour and word-play into healing tools.

His model has survived and as with all good models is constantly being revised, updated and added to by the creative practitioners who are being trained today. It forms a substantial part of Neuro Linguistic Programming (NLP). NLP is the study of success in achieving positive change which was developed in the 1970s by Richard Bandler and John Grinder.

Hypnotherapy Today

In 2003, The Wall Street Journal ran an article on how hypnosis was gaining respectability among the medical profession. The journalist, Michael Waldholz, talked about how:

- Hypnosis transformed the treatment of irritable bowel syndrome at the University of North Carolina through enabling the mind to calm the gut;

- Doctors at the University of Washington use hypnosis for pain relief in burns patients;

- Hospitals affiliated to Harvard Medical School use hypnosis to speed up post-surgical recovery time, in some cases by several weeks.

If you Google "self-hypnosis in surgery" you will find all kinds of video evidence of the surgery and dentistry taking place right now in the 21st century. With hypnosis in surgery:

- You recover more quickly

- You don't bleed excessively

- Your body doesn't have to deal with the toxic chemicals that make up chemical anesthesia.

In this chapter we have briefly explored how hypnosis and hypnotherapy developed through the ages. We will next go on to explore more of the science of the mind.

> *It's never too late to be who you might have been*
>
> **George Elliot**

3

THE SCIENCE BIT
UNDERSTANDING THE MIND

The key to understanding the science of the mind is to first of all understand how the mind and body deal with perception.

Perception is simply how we individually interpret information – this is a very personal and subconscious process:

1. We receive information through our senses.

2. We subconsciously analyse the information to form our perception.

3. The subconscious mind decides which is the best way to deal with what we are perceiving, therefore creating our reactions and responses.

So how do we do that?

The diagram which appears on page 29 is symbolic of the mind. There is proven research now that we carry memories in every cell of our body, so not just the brain affects how we respond to things. Of particular interest are 'Molecules of Emotion' by Candace B Pert, PH.D and 'The Biology of Belief' by Bruce H Lipton, PH.D.

For the purpose of this explanation the diagram illustrates the main factors we need to know.

Three concentric circles represent the mind. The outer circle represents the **conscious** mind. The middle circle the **subconscious** and the small inner circle the **unconscious** mind.

The Conscious Mind

This is the part of the mind that we use for everyday activities. Our work, our chores and socialising are generally undertaken in the normal, conscious, fully-alert, waking state.

The conscious mind is the part of the mind that contains our short-term memory, our intellect and our will-power. It enables our capacity for being logical, rational and analytical.

It can only hold a maximum of 9 bits of information at one time. So, if you overload it, information 'falls off'. For example, if you are aware of this book, you may be unaware of the temperature around you. As you become aware of the temperature around you, you may be unaware of the feeling of your hands. As you become aware of the feeling of your hands you may be unaware of the sounds outside the room. And so on. Your conscious mind can only attend to a few pieces of information at any one time and yet we are exposed to millions of pieces of information in any moment.

The conscious mind is a very well-used and very necessary part of our mind. Despite this, it is only a very small part of the mind. Most people are shocked when they find out it's only about 5% of our mind. A very small part of our brain is employed for conscious mind tasks.

YOUR MIND MAP

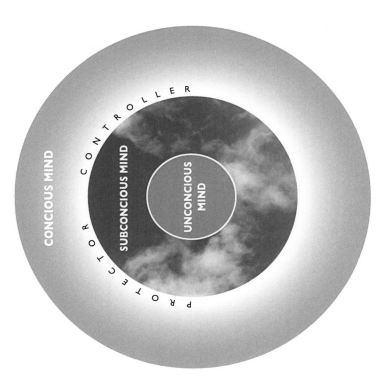

CONCIOUS MIND

SUBCONCIOUS MIND

PROTECTOR CONTROLLER

UNCONCIOUS MIND

CONSCIOUS MIND

- Past, present and future
- Rational, logical, analytical
- Only 5% of the mind
- Short term memory (5-9 items of information)
- Willpower
- Intellect

SUBCONSCIOUS MIND

- The powerhouse of the mind
- Unlimited memory
- Beliefs
- Patterns of behaviour
- Habits
- Fears and phobias

UNCONSCIOUS MIND

- Automatic body functions, ie. heart, breathing, digestion, etc

PROTECTOR CONTROLLER

- Decides what to allow into the subconscious mind
- Accessed through hypnosis

When a person insists that they are totally logical and rational, we have to remember - only 5%!

The Subconscious Mind

This is the power-house of the mind. Our subconscious mind is truly amazing - it is our control centre.

The 9 items of information, which is the absolute maximum the short-term memory can manage at one time, is a drop in the ocean for the subconscious. We have an infinite capacity to take in new information. Our subconscious remembers every second of every day, from the time we start to take in sentient memories, whilst in the womb. We log into our memory databank every second of every day we live. We're pretty impressive aren't we?

Of course, we don't need to recall more than a fraction of this information into our conscious awareness. We have all our memories of past events safely stored. These memories, whether consciously remembered or not, inform our reactions and responses to our experiences. For example, little Adam, who was bullied at the age of six, grows up and consciously forgets the experience, but subconsciously responds to assertive characters with unwarranted trepidation.

So, all the information we receive and the way we interpret it through our perception, helps to create our belief system which in turn informs our patterns of behaviour.

How we act and react is as a result of all we have seen, heard, read and experienced. Most of this serves us very well as it enables us to interact with other people, manage and plan our lives and to look after ourselves. For example, Sue, who was also bullied as a young child, learned to overcome the bullies by asserting herself and so was able to navigate conflict constructively as she grew up. This helped her in her relationships and her career.

It is therefore perfectly logical that all our **unwanted** patterns of behaviour, as we saw with Adam, and our fears and phobias, are as a result of information that has been logged into our subconscious memory banks. Since much of this information stems from our distant past, we may have no conscious memory of why or where it started. Even if we do remember the root causes, we may struggle to change our actions and reactions.

Why Change Can Be Difficult

* In hypnotherapeutic work we refer to:
* The Protector
* The Controller
* The Critical Factor

These are all names for the part of our mind which is our protection for the subconscious mind.

By about the age of 7 this protection is in place, and quite rightly. It means that we don't believe everything we are told, because the subconscious refers to what we already know, and with that in view, it accepts what is congruent with the internalized messages and rejects what is contradictory.

For example, if a mother bringing up her little toddler always tells the child the world is flat, it will believe it is flat, because it doesn't know anything else to contradict that theory. Also, from the age of 0-7, we are very open and suggestible (more of that later in the chapter when we talk about brain wave patterns). So it will only be when the child gets to school, or amongst other people, that it will learn the truth that, as in our example, the world is round.

If the information taken in is more personal and subjective, then the belief may persist throughout their entire life - even though it may be just as inaccurate. i.e. "I'm only lovable if I eat all the dinner on my plate" or "If I worry and stay on high-alert, then I'll avoid bad things happening."

Whatever we understand on an intellectual level and however hard we exercise our will-power, if the information is out of synch with our subconscious beliefs, then the Protector/Controller will edit it out and it will not cross the threshold into our subconscious mind.

Past, Present, Future or Never?

It is also very important to note that the conscious mind is the part that understands linear time - past, present and future. The reason it's so important to be aware of this is because the subconscious mind - the area of the mind we address during hypnosis - doesn't have the same concept of time.

The subconscious is always in the present - the **now** - so talking in the future tense when addressing the subconscious will **not** make it spring into action. The subconscious will think "Oh they're talking about tomorrow - no need to do anything today." For the subconscious, tomorrow never comes, there is only today, now.

The Unconscious Mind

For the purpose of this work, the unconscious mind equates to the autonomic nervous system. This is what generates and regulates the automatic functions of the body - heart beating, lungs breathing, food digesting etc. All this generally functions beautifully if left to its own devices, but the **subconscious** is the big controller, so it can alter body chemistry literally at the speed of thought.

Fight or Flight

The fight or flight principle is familiar to most of us. We think a worrying thought and our body responds. Muscles tighten, heart beats faster, we may even start to perspire or feel nauseous - this is not helpful if you are about to give a presentation, or have to finish some important work that requires calm, focus and concentration.

We still respond like our cave-dwelling ancestors, when it was a life-saving response to a real and present threat. Imagine the scene - strolling across the plain, tummy full of yummy berries and fresh spring water, just enjoying the sunshine and then, over the horizon stomps a sabre-tooth tiger. WAH!! (Caveman speak for "My goodness me, he looks dangerous!")

This fearful thought flashes through the mind and the mind flashes it's response to the physical body. We instantly secrete catecholamines (the stress hormone) which triggers the body to speed up the heart rate, send the blood supply to the arms and legs and lose any excess weight (i.e. the urge to empty the bladder and bowel), so that cave-person can run fast to find safety, or pick up their spear and shield and slay the beast.

When the blood supply goes to the arms and legs, it deprives the rest of the body of blood (blood carries nutrients, and oxygen and is an escape route for waste products), so digesting food is curtailed until calmness returns. This explains why highly-stressed people often suffer from IBS, indigestion and other problems that lie within that area of the body.

So, if the mind can affect our fear response at the speed of thought, what else might be affected in other ways, just by thoughts? There are theories that suggest all physical dis-ease is first triggered by negative emotions, not just fear, stress and worry, but also anger, disappointment, fatigue etc.

The good thing is that we can trigger more pleasurable responses by thinking happy and satisfying thoughts, which are also proven to be beneficial for our physical health.

Brain Wave Patterns

Brain waves are the electrical impulses which occur with brain activity. They influence our ability to absorb new suggestions, ideas and beliefs.

Helen Crawford, an experimental psychologist at Virginia Polytechnic Institute in Virginia, USA, showed through imaging and brain-wave measuring tools that hypnosis did indeed alter brain function.

Whilst brain waves can be measured, the ability to measure them is not necessary for self-hypnosis to occur. However, the following explanation will help you to understand what's happening during the process.

There are 4 different classifications for brain wave patterns.

1. Beta State

14 cycles to 22 cycles per second

Beta is the frequency of the conscious mind and the state in which we conduct our daily activities that involve rational, logical thinking. This is called the 'waking state'. Beta is appropriate at a meeting, talking, reasoning and thinking. When we are in an active, 'doing' state we are predominately in the beta range.

The beta frequency has been widely accepted as the least likely brain wave pattern to be receptive to suggestions.

So Beta is the state when the conscious mind is to the fore. It's great for working and living out our daily lives, but not good if we want to change how we respond to things on the subconscious level.

2. Alpha State

7 to 14 cycles per second

We go into Alpha state when the intensity of the conscious mind slows down. We are in and out of this state every day of our lives. It is normal and natural and usually very pleasant. It is the state we are in when we day dream. The same brain wave frequency happens when we dream during sleep and Rapid Eye Movement (REM) takes place.

Alpha is also that lovely state between sleeping and waking, when you know you're not asleep and can hear and be aware of all that is going on around you, but you're just too comfortable to want to open your eyes and engage with the outside world.

This is an ideal state for self-hypnosis as in this state we have direct access to the subconscious mind. During this frequency suggestions are easily absorbed.

Children between the age of 7 to 14 function predominately in this state and during these ages they are incredibly receptive to suggestions from all sources. They need to be highly suggestible in order to learn and store information quickly and easily.

You don't have to be relaxed to be suggestible, but it's the easiest and nicest way to work.

Focusing

We also enter alpha state when we focus all our attention onto something. For instance, when we watch a good film, or TV programme, read a good book or go to see a live performance.

A good performer 'entrances' the audience - the audience goes into alpha state and will be drawn in such that they become entirely focused on what they are doing or saying to the exclusion of everything else around them.

Open to Suggestion

When we are in alpha we open up our subconscious mind, which, of course, is where we hold all our memories. Our emotions are integral to our memories, so that is why we find ourselves crying over something sentimental and becoming tense and fearful when we watch a thriller.

In this state we are incredibly suggestible. Helen has lost count of how many times she's been too lazy to change the TV channel and ended up watching a really bad scary movie, but even though she knows it's pure fiction - and sometimes badly made to boot – she admits to still getting really drawn in and having to leave lights on and double check all the doors are locked!!

When we utilise visualisation as a therapeutic tool, we embrace all the power of our suggestibility in alpha state for our own benefit and positive rewards. Let's thank our wonderful imaginations! We will explore visualisation in more depth in Chapter 6.

Problem Solving

Because we are very imaginative in alpha state, we also have an incredible capacity for problem solving. The classic example of this is when we go to bed worrying about a problem that seems insurmountable, and then when we wake up in the morning, hey presto, it's no longer a problem. Sometimes we don't even remember it was an issue, we just get on and deal with it.

Creative people, writers and inventors, have, over the centuries, talked about their ideas coming to them in a dream, or a 'reverie'. This is alpha state with the creative subconscious working to its full potential.

3. Theta State

4 to 7 cycles per second

Theta is considered to be the psychic frequency of the mind, and emotional experiences are stored at this brain wave range. In the Theta state learning is extremely rapid and our imagination is incredibly strong.

If we go very deeply into self-hypnosis relaxation, then we may enter Theta state – though this is not essential for self-hypnosis to work. In Theta you may lose the awareness of what is going on around you, which is fine - just enjoy.

Children under the age of 7 predominately use this frequency and it is the most highly suggestible brain wave pattern.

4. Delta State

0 to 4 cycles per second

The delta state is when you are unconscious, when you are deeply asleep or when you are under anaesthetic. Very restful, but not useful for the purposes of self-hypnosis!

In order for the most productive self-hypnosis experience, it helps to aim for Alpha or Theta state and you will learn how to do this in the following chapter.

Any thought that is passed onto the subconscious often enough and convincingly enough is finally accepted.

Robert Collier

4

INSPIRE YOURSELF – THE FIRST LEVEL
BREATHING AND INDUCING
SELF-HYPNOSIS

SELF-HYPNOSIS

What is the first thing we do when we're born into this world? Breathe.

So why do we need to re-learn something we do every day and have done instinctively from the first day of our lives? Well, we also slept without fear, stress or any conscious concerns or worries in the first days of our lives, but can anyone say they do that every night now? If you have been motivated to read this book, then the answer is probably "no".

So, let's start from the beginning again and remind ourselves how easy it is.

Firstly, here's the science.

When we breathe out, we breathe out 70% of the body's unwanted toxins. If you thought that everything we excreted got flushed down the toilet, this may come as a surprise. So, if you think about what we would be like if we only allowed a small proportion of that waste to leave our bodies, then think also about how important it is to not only breathe in deeply, but also to breathe out fully as well.

We tend to shallow-breathe when we are stressed. It's a natural human response to hold our breath if we are frightened, shocked or caught up in a 'drama' - either real or fictional. When we only use the upper part of our lungs, which we do if we shallow-breathe, then we are depriving muscles, body tissue and the brain, of oxygen.

Oxygen is vital for our well-being. It allows the muscles to relax, the brain to function efficiently and the body to heal and cleanse itself of toxins. So, how to ensure we breathe effectively?

The Complete Breath

The best way to re-learn how to breathe effectively is to start by giving it all your attention. Then:

- Sit or lie in a comfortable position.

- Don't cross your arms or legs - you might restrict the blood flow.

- Breathe through your nose (unless you are suffering from a cold or congestion) - it makes the breath slower and more gentle.

- Draw the breath slowly and gently to the bottom of your lungs.

- Feel your abdomen pushing out. This happens because the lower lungs push the diaphragm down causing the belly to expand. (No need for flat stomachs in this exercise!)

- Feel your breath filling your lungs from the bottom to the top – it should feel as if your lungs fill up almost to your shoulders.

- Pause a moment, and then slowly exhale.

- Let your breath empty from the bottom of the lungs to the top.

As practice, you might want to try breathing in to the count of 8, pausing for the comfortable count of 4 and breathing out to the count of 8.

If you find the breathing difficult, then give yourself permission to do it in your own way. The only measure of success is what works for you. If we worry about getting things 100% correct, then the worry makes us tense and that makes breathing more difficult (more about that later). So the message here is **slow and gentle and as deep as possible**.

Now that you have mastered the complete breath, let's move on to using this as part of an induction (doorway) to hypnosis:

Induction

To induce hypnosis, simply follow these simple steps:

1. Preparation:

- Find yourself somewhere suitable to relax.

- Make sure there are no distractions. Tell people not to disturb you – this is your time.

- Switch off your phone.

- Make yourself comfortable.

2. Induction:

- Repeat the gentle complete breath exercise above, slowly filling your lungs, pausing and, equally slowly, exhaling.

- Focus on the relaxation.

- You will notice as you breathe, that your upper chest relaxes down with the exhalation. Go with that.

- As you feel your chest relaxing down, allow the rest of your body to follow.

- Feel your shoulders relaxing down.

- Allow your arms and hands to relax down - feeling heavy and relaxed and comfortable.

- Feel your legs relaxing down - feeling heavy and relaxed and comfortable.

- Imagine your feet relaxing slowly - know that your body is safe and supported, so if it feels as if it's sinking down - know that's OK and just enjoy the feeling.

- Allow your neck and throat to feel relaxed and open.

- Allow your face to relax - particularly your jaw - we often clench our teeth without even being aware of it. You might want to part your teeth slightly to relax your jaw and your tongue.

Deepening

The next phase is to deepen your relaxation which is done as follows:

1. As you breathe out, towards the end of your out-breath, start counting from the number 1 and then down to 10 - silently in your mind. **1 count on each out breath.**

2. After the count, say to yourself "deeply relaxed". Say the words in your mind slowly and languidly - no one can hear you, so if you sound like a ham actor, that's fine, only your subconscious mind is listening. Your subconscious mind will respond - it loves to be soothed! Just to be clear, this deepening will be something like this, counting at the bottom of your out-breath:

In-breath. Out-breath, count one, deeply relaxed

In-breath. Out-breath, count two, deeply relaxed

In-breath. Out-breath, count three, deeply relaxed

In-breath. Out-breath, count four, deeply relaxed

In-breath. Out-breath, count five, deeply relaxed

In-breath. Out-breath, count six, deeply relaxed

In-breath. Out-breath, count seven, deeply relaxed

In-breath. Out-breath, count eight, deeply relaxed

In-breath. Out-breath, count nine, deeply relaxed

In-breath. Out-breath, count ten, deeply relaxed

After 10 breaths and 10 counts, followed by "deeply relaxed", you'll be in a nice, gentle hypnotic trance - it really is that easy.

3. If you're having a particularly stressful time, you may want to count a little more - remember, there is no absolute right or wrong about this, do whatever works for you.

Just enjoy this hypnotic relaxation - it will also help to ground you in times of stress.

You can also make use of this time by incorporating suggestions into your self-hypnosis practice. We will be going into this in depth in the next chapter.

In the meantime, you can enjoy Level One with some simple, positive suggestions, such as:

- I'm calm and relaxed

- I am strong and confident

- Life is easy

- I love and value myself

This will bring more power to your Level One self-hypnosis practice, quite simply and quite quickly.

It is better to spend between 3 and 5 minutes in this phase. However, even if you only have one minute, you can still benefit.

Emerging

When you are ready to emerge and come back to full conscious alertness, all you need to do is count back from 10 to 1. This is done faster than in the induction to help "bring you out". On the count of 1, open your eyes and you will come back immediately to full awareness. You can count back from 10 to 1 as slowly or as quickly as you choose.

In the next chapter, you will learn the five principles of how to construct effective suggestions. Once you master these, you will be well on your way to creating positive change in your life.

> *One way to break up any kind of tension is good deep breathing.*
>
> **Byron Nelson**

5

IT'S A GOAL! - THE SECOND LEVEL
HOW TO TARGET YOURSELF
FOR SUCCESS

A question which we ask all of our clients is what goals they want to achieve from working with us. We would estimate that about 75% of people respond by telling us what they want to **avoid**. This is not at all surprising since what we focus on, we attract and focusing on the problem rather than the solution is what keeps people stuck. When people are stuck, they come to hypnotherapists like us to help them through.

When we focus on what we don't want, we get more of that, because the brain organises itself around that.

For example, if we ask you not to think of a polka-dot house, what happens? Immediately you have thoughts or images of a polka-dot house. In order to **not** focus on it, you have to first focus on it so that you know what not to focus on. With us so far? Then, some of the more enlightened people will think of perhaps something quite different such as a marshmallow river. A marshmallow river is clearly not a polka-dot house. But the polka-dot house will always appear first, because you implanted it.

Typically clients will say things like:

- I **don't** want to be left on the shelf
- I want to **avoid** any more arguments with my partner
- I **don't** want to be afraid of flying
- I want to **stop** procrastinating
- I **don't** want to be in this job for ever
- I **don't** want to rely on alcohol to feel good
- I want to **stop** eating for comfort
- I want to **avoid** blushing when I meet new people

When a mother says to her child "don't be frightened", it signals to the child that there is something to avoid being frightened of. It instils a sense of fear rather than comfort which is what the mother intends in the statement. So, what we say to ourselves, and how we say it, is really very important. Your mind is an obedient servant so do make sure you tell it what you want it to hear! If you focus most of your time on the problem and only a small percentage of your time on the "not-problem", your mind will focus on the problem. It takes focused effort to work on your goals, not a couple of affirmations when you remember. This is why self-hypnosis can be so powerful.

The best way to get rid of negative thoughts is to replace them with positive ones. This is where suggestions, or affirmations, come in.

Hypnosis, as already discussed, is composed of several steps:

1. Induction

This is the First Level.

2. Deepening

This is also included in the First Level.

3. Hypnosis Techniques for Positive Change

This is what we are going to cover in this and subsequent chapters. This is covered in Levels Two, Three and Four.

4. Emerging

Bringing you back into conscious awareness.

An Inside Job Self-Hypnosis™ includes three options for the hypnosis part of the process and you can use one, two or all three for a more powerful effect.

This chapter is The Second Level which covers the goals, or affirmations (also known as suggestions) that you will be using. It is the simplest form of self-hypnosis and helps you target yourself for success. Imagine a marksman aiming for the bulls-eye in his target, but looking at the beautiful scenery either side. What is he going to hit? The scenery. It is only if he focuses on the bulls-eye and only the bulls-eye that he hits it - unless of course, he is remarkably lucky! But self-hypnosis is not about relying on luck. It is an opportunity to take charge of what you want from yourself and your life. So make sure you are clear about your target and you are more likely to get what you want so that you can create affirmations that work for your subconscious and help effect positive change.

Here are the basic rules:

1. Be Creative

You can be creative with your affirmations, designing them to suit what you want to improve in your life. They can be general, feel-good suggestions, or something more specific to help you achieve your goals in life.

2. Be Positive

Remember that the subconscious will respond to your words, so **never** make a negative affirmation, you **always** make a positive one. Otherwise, you will find yourself automatically and instinctively heading towards fulfilling that negative.

The subconscious is naturally **goal-seeking**, so trust it to follow your instructions - it wants to know where to take you.

3. Keep Affirmations Short and Simple

Think of your subconscious like a cross between a wise professor and a 5-year old child. We all have great inner wisdom and, when we access the subconscious, as you are when doing this simple self-hypnosis, then you create a direct connection to that wisdom.

If you talk to the subconscious as you talk to a young child – in a nurturing tone with a sense of conviction - then it will respond more effectively. Keeping things simple avoids ambiguity which can confuse the subconscious.

4. **Say it Like You Mean It**

   Your subconscious mind is open to affirmations if
   you speak with calm conviction. When you act as
   though the affirmation is true, even if you don't
   quite believe it yet, it will absorb the affirmation
   as though it **is** true. If you sound as if you don't
   believe the affirmation, your subconscious won't
   either. Your subconscious is your obedient
   servant – make sure it works for you.

5. **Keep it in the Present Tense**

   The reason it's important to say things in the
   present tense is that the subconscious doesn't
   understand the concept of past, present and
   future. Linear thinking is done in the conscious
   mind, whereas the subconscious is always in
   the **now**.

   As we have discussed in Chapter 3, if you say
   "I **will be** calm and relaxed", then the
   subconsious will think "Oh, that means
   tomorrow, so I don't need to do anything about
   it now" and it won't ever address the issue
   because it will always see it as a future issue
   and it's never in the future, only in the now.
   To be effective, the affirmation would have to
   be modified to "I **am** calm and relaxed".

With An Inside Job ™ Self-Hypnosis you are reprogramming
yourself. The more you do it, the quicker you will get the
results. But, unlike other programs, it acknowledges where you
are now. Normally, when we repeat an affirmation we have
a subconscious answer which can be negative, as if we don't

believe the affirmation yet, because, of course, it isn't true yet. By acknowledging this, it enables the process to progress organically. By repeating the affirmation, you will be reducing the strength of any negative response.

Affirmation Responses

It's also important to realise that some of the responses may not be directly related to the affirmation. This is OK – let your mind respond with whatever comes up. There are three levels of response:

Negative   The response negates the affirmations. However, the effect will be neutral because a plus and a minus cancel each other out (remember this from your school days?)

Neutral   The response has a neutral effect on the affirmation. The effect, however, is positive because when you add nothing to a positive, you still have a positive.

Positive   The response supports the affirmation so you get a double positive.

Let's look at an example of how it all works with an affirmation about confidence – a common goal for clients:

AFFIRMATION	RESPONSE	RESPONSE TYPE	RESPONSE EFFECT
I am confident	But I'm not!	Negative	Neutral
I am confident	I'm anything but confident	Negative	Neutral
I am confident	No-one could ever describe me as confident	Negative	Neutral
I am confident	No-one has ever described me as confident	Neutral	Positive
I am confident	No-one has ever described me as confident	Neutral	Positive
I am confident	If I'm so confident why am I single?	Negative	Neutral
I am confident	What shall I buy Julia for her birthday?	Neutral	Positive
I am confident	Shall we go out to dinner rather than cook?	Neutral	Positive
I am confident	If I'm truly confident, why am I in a dead-end job?	Negative	Neutral

AFFIRMATION	RESPONSE	RESPONSE TYPE	RESPONSE EFFECT
I am confident	Well, I suppose I was with that awkward customer yesterday.	Positive	Positive
I am confident	I am confident when it comes to helping someone in need	Positive	Positive
I am confident	I was confident meeting the new person at work	Positive	Positive
I am confident	I am confident	Positive	Positive
I am confident	I am confident	Positive	Positive
I am confident	I am confident and it feels great	Positive	Positive

There may not be a flow from negative to neutral to positive. This is perfectly fine. Simply allow things to flow naturally. It is important that you don't force this process in any way for this to be effective.

Repetition of the affirmation and the response is essential. It won't work if you simply repeat the affirmation over and over and notice your response at the end. The power is in the affirmation-response-affirmation-response-affirmation-response pattern.

If your goal is to be confident and you are not confident, it is going to take a while for the positive program to override all the negative programming which has been going on for years. By allowing your natural response and following it with the positive affirmation, you are in effect neutralising or diluting the negative. Resisting the negative simply serves to make it stronger. By acknowledging it and following it with your affirmation, over time, the negative will be the one which is false and the positive will become the one which is true.

Another thing will happen. Your responses will become more positive thereby re-enforcing the affirmation, so you are getting an even stronger impact.

Your affirmation can be anything which is stated in the positive which you want to be true for you.

Levels of Affirmation

Before you begin, let's look at the levels at which you could aim your affirmations and the effect this has. Neuro Linguistic Programming (NLP) looks at the concept of Logical Levels. These are the levels of experience and affirmations can be set at any level, all of which have a different impact on your subconscious mind. The levels include:

1. Spiritual
2. Identity
3. Belief
4. Capability
5. Behaviour
6. Environment

Let's say that you want to be more patient and compassionate. The following table includes descriptions of each of the levels and examples of how affirmations might be worded for each of them.

LEVEL	DESCRIPTION	EXAMPLE AFFIRMATION
Spiritual	Your purpose	I bring patience and compassion to people's lives
Identity	Who you are – your core self.	I am patience and compassion
Belief	What you believe to be true	Being patient and compassionate makes life less stressful
Capability	Your skills	I am good at being patient and compassionate

Behaviour	What you do	I am patient and compassionate towards the vulnerable
Environment	Your response to your environment	I am patient and compassionate at work

Clearly, the affirmations which will have the biggest impact in your overall life will be the Spiritual and Identity levels because they are influencing you from the inside, at your very core, rather than being a conscious effort or conditional on other factors as implied by the other levels.

Affirmation Examples

Here are some affirmations to help you along the way. These are quite general so you may want to tailor them to meet your specific needs but they are a good starting point:

Self-Esteem

- I choose to love and accept myself
- I see, acknowledge and appreciate the goodness in me
- I am enough, just as I am
- I deserve and allow myself to (your goal)
- I deeply and completely accept myself without judgement
- I am worthy
- I am important
- I deserve to be happy

- I am OK as I am
- I am strong
- I am capable
- I allow myself to succeed
- I'm a powerful, unique and special person
- It's safe to succeed

Stress

- Each day is a new beginning emotionally, physically and spiritually
- Life is easy
- I allow myself to be human
- I develop through challenge
- I allow good things to happen to me
- It is safe to be me
- My best is good enough
- I release all negative emotion
- I have nothing to fear (one of the few negative affirmations which work)

Loneliness

- I am connected to myself, to others and the world
- I make friends easily
- People warm to me
- I enjoy being with people

Relationships

- I have collaborative, supportive and respectful relationships with myself and others
- I am loved and loveable
- I attract supportive friends
- It is safe to be loved
- I can choose whom I trust
- I am attractive

Inner Peace

- I am patience and compassion
- I am patient, compassionate and assertive
- I live life with a full heart and an open mind
- I release myself from the past
- I release the past, enjoy the present and look forward to the future
- I am at peace with myself, with others, and the world
- (God*) guides and supports me
- I live my life with grace and ease
- I enjoy each moment and each new moment of now
- I am connected to (God*)
  *Or your concept of your Highest Power such as Spirit, Love, Family, the Universe, etc?

Health

- My body systems are strong and in balance

- My body heals and repairs itself
- My cells are functioning perfectly
- My organs enjoy vibrant health
- I love to exercise
- I give myself permission to heal
- I am energised, healthy and strong

Goal Achievement

- I choose to (goal)
- I work diligently and enthusiastically towards (goal)
- Every day I am becoming more and more (goal)
- I have free will and choice to (goal)
- My choices empower me
- I am successful and respected

Abundance

- I allow myself to thrive
- I am worthy and deserving of abundance
- I have everything I need
- I manifest abundance
- Good things come to me
- It is safe to be rich
- I attract good, appreciative customers
- I allow money to flow to me

Forgiveness

- I forgive myself my mistakes
- I forgive others their mistakes
- I let go of resentment
- I forgive myself for my past – I am not my past
- I forgive myself for being so hard on myself
- I forgive myself for being so hard on (name)
- I forgive myself for my judgements
- I forgive (name) for their judgments
- I am forgiveness

General

- I learn and grow from mistakes, both mine and others'
- I create my world and my life
- I am empowered to make positive choices
- I have the power of choice in thought, action and deed
- I deserve and allow myself to be happy
- I am a positive example to others
- All my experiences enhance and enrich me
- I am resourceful and resilient
- I am safe
- I am intelligent
- I trust my own judgement
- I can safely feel my emotions

- I can make my needs known

- I have choice and freewill

These are examples – you can use whatever affirmations, or suggestions, you want. Be creative, but always be positive. You will notice that words such as "I choose …", "I deserve …", "It's safe to …" and "I allow …" are used in some of them. They are just options – choose whatever works for you. Mix and match as you see fit.

Do remember that if you resist the negative responses, they persist. Your negative voice wants to be heard. This system allows you to acknowledge it. The more you resist it, the more it will shout out to be noticed and the greater will be the negative effect on you.

You can acknowledge your negative voice **and** make choices for something different. By making positive choices, you are creating new, positive habits.

A bad habit, Horace Mann, the American education reformer once said, is like a cable. We weave a thread of it every day until it becomes so strong, it can't be broken. However, by repeating the suggestions, you are making them true for you and you are diluting the effectiveness of the negative (unravelling the cable) whilst creating what you want. You are becoming the creator of your own reality, breaking bad habits and creating new, positive ones.

To be clear, repetition is key. It takes a long time to form a bad habit, repetition of the positive suggestion is essential. Set yourself several minutes to repeat the suggestion in your self-hypnosis practice and do this for as many days as you need to until you have formed your new way of being.

Acknowledging the negative voice whilst making choices creates your future:

You can be angry **and** forgive

You can want chocolate and **choose** to say no to it

You can be aware of the past **and** decide to live in the present

You can enjoy a lie-in and **choose** to get up and make a start on the decorating

You can be right in an argument and **choose** to forgive the other

Ridding yourself of a bad habit is difficult unless you replace it with a positive one. So choose wisely. Select affirmations which are self-affirming and conducive to the life you want to create for yourself.

The optimum length of time to spend on this phase is between 5-10 minutes. If time is short, even one minute will help.

In summary:

1. Be positive

2. Use the present tense

3. Keep it short and simple

4. Say it like you mean it

5. Allow your natural response

6. Return to the suggestion

Repeat the 'affirmation-response' cycle for the duration of this phase of your self-hypnosis practice

In the next chapter, you will learn how to use visualisation to help your self-hypnosis practice be even more powerful still.

> *Watch your thoughts, for they become words*
> *Watch your words, for they become actions*
> *Watch your actions, for they become habits*
> *Watch your habits, for they become character*
> *Watch your character, for it becomes your destiny*
>
> **Frank Outlaw**

6

SEEING IS BELIEVING - THE THIRD LEVEL
THE ART OF VISUALISATION IN ACHIEVING CHANGE

Visualisation has an important role to play in helping you to make the changes you want in your life, whatever they are. The astounding effects of visualisation in achieving transformative change were highlighted in some research undertaken with a Soviet team who were preparing for the 1980 Olympics.

The group was split into four:

1. Group one undertook their normal physical training.

2. Group two did their normal physical training for 75% of the time and added in 25% of visualisation techniques.

3. Group three did their normal physical training for 50% of the time and the remaining 50% of the time did visualisation.

4. Group four did their normal physical training 25% of the time but spent 75% of the time in visualisation.

You may expect that those who dedicated themselves more fully to physical practice would have enjoyed the greatest performance improvement. But you would be wrong. The group whose performance improved the most, were those who did only 25% physical training and spent the rest of the time visualising their success.

This is fantastic news since visualisation is so easy to incorporate into daily life and into your An Inside Job™ Self-Hypnosis practice.

Most people visualise themselves as they **don't** want to be. Then they are surprised they find it difficult to make changes. For example:

- Sally wanted to be slim but her mind's eye could only picture her pouring out of the top of her too-tight jeans whilst munching on huge slabs of chocolate.

- Graham wanted to be a successful salesman but he visualised himself in his current job as a call-centre consultant, unhappy and bored.

- Anna wanted to be confident but could only picture herself on the outside of any social gathering, head bowed, mouth turned down and always in black and white, whilst she pictured others in full technicolour glory, smiling and vibrant.

By using visualisation for what you **do** want, richly, using all your senses (auditory - hear, visual - see and kinaesthetic - feel) you can help your mind prepare for, create and accept change.

Let's take a few examples.

David

David was doing very well in his career. He worked in a large company in telesales and was promoted to an external sales role where, as well as the hefty salary increase, he was given commission and a company car. Life was good! But along with all the benefits, he was required to do one thing which he hated (one of life's greatest fears) – presenting. Whilst he was a sociable person who liked interacting with others and had good people skills, he was really nervous about standing up in front of a bunch of executives and going through a Powerpoint presentation.

So let's see what movie he was playing in his mind's eye to 'help' him:

See	• He is hunched over, eyes down • Perspiration beads his brow • The audience look bored and are looking at their watches as if they have somewhere better to be
Hear	• His voice is dull and hesitant • There are gaps between words as he struggles to remember the points, even though they are right there on the Powerpoint presentation
Feel	• He feels anxious and full of dread, as though he would prefer, like his audience, to be anywhere else in the world but here • His palms are sweaty • His breathing is shallow • His hands are shaking and he stuffs them into his pockets to hide this, jangling his loose change to distract himself

This kind of visualisation is like a dress rehearsal for failure. He was getting his brain set up to focus on exactly the behaviours he didn't want to experience.

Here is a good and empowering visualisation for David:

See	• He is standing tall in front of a room full of people • The people are looking at him, interested in what he is saying, nodding in parts • His gestures are relaxed and enhance his presentation • He looks completely at ease and is engaging the audience with good eye contact
Hear	• He can hear his voice strong and confident • The words are flowing easily and effortlessly with appropriate pauses to enhance the points he wants to make • The audience are asking him good questions which enable him to show his expertise • He hears their applause, loud and appreciative at the end of the presentation
Feel	• He feels calm and strong • His hands are cool and relaxed and use gestures which emphasise his points • His breathing is steady and deep

Can you see how this would bring about a more positive result for David? What you think about you bring about. By visualising how he wanted to be, his mind organised itself, his thoughts, feelings and behaviours, to recreate the visualisation that his mind had rehearsed for him.

Emma

Now let's take another example. Emma had been trying to lose weight for a couple of years but just couldn't lose more than a pound or two and put it straight back on, plus some. She was getting bigger and bigger. Her beautiful, trendy clothes no longer fitted her and she was having to buy 'fat' clothes which made her feel ugly. She felt so low that she just ate more and more and, of course, felt worse and worse. This is what was going on for Emma in terms of her visualisation:

See	• Herself in her 'fat' clothes, looking huge and really unhappy • Seeing herself alone and lonely watching a film with chocolates and cakes for company

Hear	• Her self-talk:
	  – "I'm so fat"
	  – "I'll always be alone"
	  – "No-one will find me attractive"
	  – "One cake should cheer me up"
	  – "I'll just have another one"

Feel	• The feeling of the fat spilling over the top of her trousers • The waistband tight and uncomfortable • The feeling of deep sorrow and loneliness in her tummy

In this visualisation Emma is focusing on her shape, her unhappiness and her eating. So, of course, her mind organises itself to make sure she stays overweight, unhappy and that she eats plenty of food, just like she rehearsed in her mind.

This keeps her firmly stuck in exactly the place she doesn't want to be.

To change this, Emma needs to change the images, sounds and feelings that she has around her life, her eating and her weight. Here is an example:

See	• Herself at the gym chatting to her new boyfriend after a good workout
	• She is wearing a great gym outfit which emphasises her trim frame
	• She looks happy and confident
Hear	• Her new boyfriend is saying that, despite her being hot and sweaty after her workout, she still looks great
	• They are both laughing
Feel	• She feels really happy that she had a great workout – every time she can do more than the last and she feels proud about her progress
	• Trim, flexible and enjoying the comfort of the size 10 clothes on her slender frame
	• Confidence which she feels from her tummy and it spreads right through her body
	• At ease with her new man – it feels really natural

In the second visualisation Emma is focusing on how happy and trim she is and this is associated with the enjoyment of exercise. There is nothing about food because her life has become more than food. Remember that what you focus on, you attract, so for Emma, focusing on her new life, trim and happy is what helped her. If she had focused on food, food would have been uppermost in her mind. An alternative visualisation might be that she is enjoying a fun evening with friends and has left food on her plate because she is full and enjoying the evening.

Jane

Let's see one more example. Jane has been having a difficult time in her relationship with Steve. They have been together 10 years. The shine has worn off and they aren't getting on – they argue about the smallest things and she is considering divorce even though she loves him deep down.

This is the scenario Jane plays to herself:

See	• Her angry face as she shouts at Steve, throwing their wedding photo on the floor • Steve looking furious and storming out of the room
Hear	• The angry words she shouts at Steve • Her self-talk — "He doesn't care" — "I won't let him win"
Feel	• Rage • Tension in her fists, face and chest

Jane's scenario increases her rage because she is focusing on what annoys her. To bring about a sense of peace and harmony in her relationship, this is what she needs to picture. Here is an example:

See	• Herself with Steve on the sofa, cuddling up as they enjoy a film together • They both look relaxed and contented and he is stroking her arm whilst she has her head on his shoulder
Hear	• Their gentle breathing, in time with each other • A contented voice in her head saying "This is nice"
Feel	• Calm, peaceful contentment

Can you see how the second "recording" Jane plays to herself will completely change how she interacts with Steve? We can't change other people, but we can change ourselves. So, by changing how she is with Steve, Steve will be much more likely to change towards her. She will start to feel this calm, peaceful contentment. They will start to relate to each other in a more positive way. What you think about, you bring about.

Your Turn

Now, think about what reality you want to make for yourself and see whether your pictures, sounds and feelings facilitate that possibility or do they get in the way of what you want?

Finally, map out, as we have above, what it would be useful for you to see, hear and feel in order to bring about a different reality.

As already mentioned, practice makes perfect and so repetition is absolutely key. The great thing is that positive visualisation is an enjoyable experience, so it makes it all the easier to do. Enjoy!

Visualisation is one of the most powerful tools of self-hypnosis. The next session, the fourth level, also very powerful, helps you to deal with any internal conflict you might be experiencing.

> *Humans are **producers** of their life circumstances, not just **products** of them.*
>
> **Albert Bandura**
> **Psychologist**

7

ALL THAT I AM – THE FOURTH LEVEL
HOW TO RECONCILE
INNER CONFLICT

Have you ever had the experience of wanting one thing, yet your actions seem to seek out something else entirely? Such as wanting desperately to lose weight, but succumbing to cravings for chocolate? Or wanting to make it up with your partner after an argument, but finding yourself making snide comments instead?

These are states of inner conflict. It can feel like you have your foot on the brake and the accelerator at the same time.

This inner conflict is caused by what we call "parts". In this context, we aren't referring to parts of the physical body, but parts of the inner self.

We all understand that we have different aspects, or facets, to our personality. We can be happy or sad, kind or unfeeling, depending on our circumstances. A sunny day and a meaningful compliment or a success, can bring an instant feeling of well-being, but this doesn't mean that the part of us that feels sadness or depression doesn't exist. It just means that one part has taken a more predominant role at that moment.

At any one time, there may be a part that predominates.

If we find that the negative aspects of us are predominating and we don't like those feelings, we need to redress the balance and bring back the more positive feelings - or instruct those parts to become stronger and more dominant.

> For instance - little Darren would love to learn to ride a bicycle, but he saw his friend fall off a bike, graze his leg and cry. Darren's **fear part** keeps coming forward, so he avoids getting on a bike for the first time. If his **success part** was encouraged to come forward, which reminds him how he jumps on swings, roundabouts and see-saws without a second thought, he would no doubt jump on a bicycle and learn to ride it too.

Parts Therapy

Parts therapy appears in many guises - inner dialogue, sub-personalities, modalities, ego-states - there are many different ways of working with the same principle. Most psychological therapies acknowledge the principle of parts and the following explanation is one way of working with them.

The over-riding factor is that whatever therapy you are undertaking, working with parts work can be powerful, revealing and potentially life-changing.

We are born with a myriad of different parts. They are all there to serve us, to get our needs met and look after our best interests. They are wonderful and essential, but potentially problematic if they get too strong or become too suppressed — in other words, if they get out of balance.

The perfect alignment of parts enables us to be balanced, successful and happy. They are like an orchestra that needs a conductor to keep the rhythm, timing and harmony under control for the symphony to be effective and wonderful to listen to. The different instruments are all making different sounds in different ways, so they could become a discordant noise, but they can blend together harmoniously if the conductor does his job well.

It's the same with a garden, if we want to make a beautiful vista that's pleasing to be in, we need to keep down weeds, feed the plants that need nourishment to grow, plant new things you choose to put in and prune plants that are too vigorous. You know how you want it to look, so you put in the work that leads to that end result. It becomes your creation. So when you decide how you want to be, you adjust the parts appropriately to create the **you** that you want to be.

Parts that Become too Powerful

Sometimes parts that develop can become like brambles that grow fast and furiously over other shrubs, or like the timpani in an orchestra that can dominate the sounds of other instruments. Now is the time for us to be our own gardeners or conductors.

We can recognise and name our **parts** in our own way, but there are some basic parts that all of us will recognise and that invariably love to be strong and powerful.

The Inner Critic

Much recognised as the little (or sometimes very loud) voice in the back of your consciousness that berates you for getting something wrong, for not being as good as you think you should be, or for any perceived misdemeanor.

In balance with the other parts, it is an excellent tool for helping us to improve in whatever we do - to enable us to succeed. So, like all other parts, it has a very valuable role to play and deserves respect.

When out of balance, it can stop you from even trying to succeed.

The Pleaser

The Pleaser, as the title suggests, pleases other people. Looking after other people is a wonderful thing to do. It can be fulfilling and rewarding. We love and respect pleasers, but if this part gets too strong it can be destructive. If we focus all our time and energy on others we will be neglecting ourselves. If we neglect ourselves we diminish our energy, we may feel unwell or aggrieved and become not only unhappy, but less able to care for others.

If the Pleaser becomes too strong we are giving our subconscious mind the message that we don't matter, we have no value - only others deserve care. It is important to change that message.

We need to respect ourselves as well as others. Sometimes the Pleaser part needs to learn to say "no" to others and give us some TLC instead.

The Perfectionist

Seeking to improve and aiming to be the best we can is an excellent quality. However, sometimes we expect more than 100% of ourselves - which of course is impossible. The tendency to have higher expectations than is mentally and physically possible seems to be a dis-ease of the 21st Century. Of course it's good to push ourselves and find our potential, but if it makes us constantly frustrated and unhappy, then it is diminishing our quality of life - not enhancing it.

So if you have an overactive Perfectionist, then maybe you need to cut yourself some slack, accept that you are OK doing your best - the world will not fall about your ears if you don't constantly achieve 100% perfection. And that 110% doesn't exist anyway - per cent means parts of 100, so how can it?

The Pusher

Are you someone who makes lots of lists - things to do or things to buy? That's your Pusher working. It drives us to achieve and succeed. We wouldn't get anywhere in life without a Pusher - it's wonderful.

Needless to say, there is the other angle. Do you also worry or agonise because you haven't completed the tasks on your list, or maybe even - heaven forbid - not started them because of competing demands. That's the Pusher in overdrive, and if it's in overdrive - time to tone it down.

Parts in overdrive feed the inner critic and the inner critic loves to be fed.

What do we Suppress?

Suppressed parts are usually the parts that don't serve us well within our family or society.

Anger

We generally learn from the 'terrible twos' onwards that showing anger is not considered acceptable behaviour. Sometimes we learn that lesson so well that we become incapable of recognising when we experience anger at all.

If someone comes for therapy and says that they never get angry, rather than thinking 'what a lovely person', the important question is 'why?'.

Anger, like every other emotion we feel, is there for a reason, it's letting us know that something is wrong with our life in some way. If, for example, someone, or something, is treating us (or someone we care about) unfairly, we have a **right** to feel anger. The lesson should be to recognise the anger, respect it and then decide how we want to redress whatever imbalance has created that anger. It's rarely productive to shout and scream: a calm assertiveness in addressing the problem in whatever way will be successfully productive is more constructive.

Suppressing or repressing anger will inevitably bring about emotional or physical dis-ease. If solutions cannot be found, then letting go of the anger is the best option.

Other Unacceptable Parts

Other unacceptable parts can stem from anything that we learn from life experiences. Helen once knew a little boy who was very much a 'boy', but was also fascinated by dolls. When he was playing with a little girl who lived nearby he loved to play with her toys and asked his daddy for a doll's pram for his birthday. Daddy was not amused. He was horrified that his son should be so un-macho. Judo and football followed. The little boy never played with dolls again and when he grew up he went into the army.

That little boy learned very fast what was 'acceptable' and 'unacceptable' behaviour. However, interestingly, he always loved children and babies and is now the proud father of 2 little girls and godfather to several more. His suppressed part was finally able to surface in a healthy way, but some parts never again see the light of day.

How many of us say "I've always wanted to draw and paint" or "play an instrument" or "walk in the Himalayas". We generally follow what we think is 'sensible' and 'right' for our chosen life and future, but what stops us from exploring our earlier passions in some way?

How Can Parts Be Balanced?

Here is a simple exercise that is fun to do. It's often illuminating and can bring about powerful and positive changes by balancing the parts in conflict with each other that consequently create discord in your life.

I. Name the Problematic Part

Before you start you may want to consider what the most problematic part is for you at this very moment and give it a name. For example:

- Inner Critic
- Not Good Enough Part
- Procrastination Part
- Anxiety Part
- Over-eating Part
- Fear of Failure Part
- Or anything else you want to work on.

2. Name the Balancing Part

Think of the part that would balance the problematic part. It may be the opposite, but not necessarily. For example:

Inner Critic	Nurturing Part
Not Good Enough Part	Confidence Part
Procrastination Part	Do It Now Part
Anxiety Part	Calm and Relaxed Part
Over-eating Part	Satisfied Part
Fear of Failure Part	Success Part

Now for the Practice

1. Sit comfortably and breathe yourself into a light Alpha state (see chapter 3). Alpha state is that feeling between sleeping and waking – where you are conscious of everything but very relaxed. Put your hands in your lap and turn the palms uppermost in a comfortable, cupped position.

2. Gaze into your least dominant hand. Usually this is the left if you're right-handed or the right hand if you are left-handed. You may close your eyes and imagine gazing into that hand if you prefer.

3. Give your imagination free rein and imagine that you are taking the most Problematic Part of you out from your subconscious mind in symbolic form and sitting it in that hand.

    Whatever comes into your imagination is fine. It may be a definite image, or maybe just a colour, texture, shape or feeling. It is often worth checking whether you sense it as light or heavy, warm or cold, soft or hard. Give yourself time to really focus on what it's like.

4. Either silently in your mind, or out loud if you prefer, welcome this part, thank it for coming forward and appreciate it. Remember - all parts think they are doing their best for you, but sometimes they are working from old, outdated messages and information. By respecting that part, you are encouraging it's participation

5. Ask that part "If I could give you anything in the whole wide world, what would you like from me, or what do you need?" Remember this is from you – no-one else. We cannot control others only ourselves.

6. Wait to hear or feel whatever comes into you mind. There is no right or wrong - only perception. Just allow whatever comes to mind rather than force something from your conscious mind.

7. When you've listened to your Problematic Part, thank it for it's co-operation and then turn your attention to your other hand.

8. Follow the same procedure with the Balancing part that you did with the Problematic Part. Imagine this one in your dominant hand. How does it appear? What colour is it? What shape? What texture etc. Is it light or heavy? Hot or cold? Does it have any distinguishing features?

9. Welcome and thank it.

10. Ask that part "If I could give you anything in the whole wide world, what would you like from me, or what do you need?"

11. Wait to hear or sense whatever comes into you mind. Again, there is no right or wrong - only perception.

12. Then ask the Balancing Part if it knows about the Problematic Part. If it doesn't — tell it what it needs to know. Then ask it if it's prepared to work with the Problematic Part.

   • If it agrees, say thank you and take your focus back to the Problematic Part.

   • If it's reluctant, use your powers of negotiation and persuasion. If necessary, let it know that this is what you really want and that it will be the very best thing for you if they work together.

   • Thank it.

13. With your focus now on the Balancing Part, repeat the process. Ask the Balancing Part if it knows about the

Problematic Part. If it doesn't — tell it what it needs to know. Then ask it if it's prepared to work with the Problematic Part.

- As previously, if it agrees, say thank you and take your focus back to the Problematic Part.

- If it's reluctant, use your powers of negotiation and persuasion. If necessary, let it know that this is what you really want and that it will be the very best thing for you if they work together.

- Thank it.

14. Then turn the process over to your subconscious. Turn your hands to face each other - palm to palm.

15. When it feels appropriate, bring your hands together and draw them towards you until both palms are flat against your solar plexus (below the heart and above your lower abdomen).

16. Allow the parts to integrate back into you - now working together in harmony.

17. Emerge. Bring your attention back to the world around you and let your subconscious carry on assimilating the healing message you have given. Open your eyes if they aren't already open.

That's it — well done! Notice any change in your feelings over the next few days. You should find that life feels easier and less fraught.

It really is a very simple process where you are respecting the needs of individual parts of your psyche and looking for ways to help them to help you in a way which is respectful of each and every part of you. To illustrate in more depth how this is done, here are a few examples:

Jennie

Jennie began to suffer from eczema whilst going through a very stressful experience that lasted a couple of years. She was in her 40's and couldn't understand why a skin condition should manifest at this stage of her life, when she'd never suffered from it before.

Her skin was unbearably itchy and inflamed and then began to split and bleed. Even when it was sore and painful, it still itched and irritated.

1. Jennie chose her Problem Part to be, of course, the **Eczema** Part. She saw it as a mini version of her. It writhed in her hand. The skin was completely flayed, burning and itching at the same time, and she imagined it with a face that was ugly and grimacing. She realised it was very angry. (It's interesting to note that when we talk about inflamed or red skin we often use the term 'angry'.)

2. She had already thought that the Balancing Part would be her **Nurturing** Part, but the poignancy of this little writhing figure instigated a spontaneous desire to send some healing. She imagined a shower of white, healing light flowing over the figure and cooling the skin. The figure stopped writhing and the face stopped grimacing. She realized that this was her **Pleaser** Part that had looked after everyone else and had no-one looking after it's needs. She had neglected herself, and the part was angry

and needed to be acknowledged. When we are angry it's because something is unfair or out of balance in our lives, so we need to listen and give ourselves consideration and respect.

3. The **Nurturing** Part appeared as a smooth clear glass sphere. There was no negotiation needed. The parts were already starting to work together. All that had been required was to give the parts attention, recognition and validation.

4. This provided Jennie with a powerful message that she should be loving and caring for herself and not always focusing on the people around her to support them. She realised she needed support too.

Having come to that realisation, she gave herself more time to relax and also sought more therapy to support her through that difficult time. The eczema reduced dramatically and eventually cleared completely.

This also illustrates that anger can manifest in many different ways and sometimes we don't even realise that it **is** anger.

Michael

Michael was aware that he needed to address his **Anger** Part. It was affecting his marriage and his work. His manager had hinted at his occasional bad attitude in his last work appraisal and Michael knew he couldn't ignore it anymore.

1. He imagined the **Anger** Part as black in colour. As he focused on it he realised it was round, quite hot in his hand and very heavy.

2. When asked what it needed or wanted from him he became aware of a feeling of tiredness. The part was tired, it wanted to rest and find peace. It also made him aware that it came forward when he was unsure of himself. It was covering up what he really felt - which was **not good enough.** At times when he felt he wasn't doing a good enough job, or not getting things right, he became angry with himself, but directed his anger at others. He thanked the part for all its hard work - this had been a very hard-working part, and already the part started to lighten and become cooler. It is often powerful for the part just to be acknowledged and respected.

3. He then knew that the Balancing Part needed was his **Calm and Confident** Part. He got an image of a beautiful sunny day, with blue sky and a peaceful, pastoral scene.

4. After thanking this part, he again asked what it wanted or needed. This part asked to be used more. It felt overshadowed and under-used. It let him know that the **Anger** Part had been one of the parts that overshadowed it. It reminded him that he was intelligent and competent and that if only he could relax and believe that, life would be altogether easier.

5. Negotiations ensued whereby the **Anger** Part was persuaded that by giving some of its powerful energy to the **Calm and Confident** Part, it would be able to relax and rest more easily. Energy can be converted from negative to positive and the **Calm and Confident** Part eventually accepted that if it was given more energy then it would have more strength to become a more powerful member in Michael's family of parts.

After the exercise, Michael felt very calm. He has a stronger awareness of why he felt anger and also a trust that he can safely allow his calmness and confidence to take a stronger place in his life, even, and especially, when problems arise.

Louise

Louise had been trying to lose weight for years. She would diet, lose weight, fall 'off the wagon' and put more on than she lost. She was becoming more and more depressed. Her biggest downfall was chocolate. She was struggling to keep up at work and would always reach for the chocolate as her way of 'coping'. But it was actually making her miserable and even more stressed. She went through the process:

1. Louise's **Overeating** Part filled her whole hand. It was dark with an indistinguishable shape. It felt hot and spiky and like it wanted to be noticed.

2. It had a voice – soft but insistent. "I need comfort". This part wanted to give Louise comfort when she was stressed and overworked. It was trying to help her deal with the stress of her job.

3. She asked what it wanted and it said "chocolate". Clearly this part knew what it wanted! Louise asked it what it was that it felt chocolate did for her. "It makes her feel calm and relaxed". She thanked it and turned her attention to the other hand.

4. She called on the **Calm and Relaxed** Part. It was round and pink and felt warm. Whereas **Overeating** Part was spiky, **Calm and Relaxed** Part was smooth.

5. Its voice was soothing "It'll be OK", "Just do what you can".

6. Asked what the **Calm and Relaxed** part wanted it said "to be consulted before she decides to have chocolate".

7. Overeating part was not happy. She had been doing her job for years and wasn't about to give up now. She had an important role to play! What would she do if she didn't do this? Discussions resulted in **Overeating** Part agreeing that it could transform itself to **Healthy Eating** Part. It agreed to be used only as a way of refueling and giving Louise healthy foods that reduced her stress rather than reach for chocolate as a way of managing emotion. It decided to change its colour to green, smooth away the spikes and change its inner dialogue from "I need comfort" to "Am I physically hungry?" This enabled her to distinguish between physical hunger and emotional hunger so she could make an informed choice over her eating.

8. Louise learned that by listening to the **Calm and Relaxed** Part she could soothe her emotions far better than a transient bar of chocolate. She realised at the deepest level that chocolate actually increased her stress and that by looking after herself and listening to her body she was better able to deal with the demands placed upon her.

Even though we might know that balance is the key to happiness and well-being, sometimes it is easy to lose sight of how to keep the balance and what we really need. This can be an interesting exercise to find out what we need and start re-balancing.

This chapter is about Level 4 – Dealing with Inner Conflict. This completes all facets of your An Inside Job™ Self-Hypnosis practice. In the next chapter, we will summarise everything for you.

> *The greatest conflicts are not between two people but between one person and himself.*
>
> **Garth Brooks**

8

SUMMARY

Change has to be An Inside Job™. When you accept that you are response-able for change – that is to say, you are in charge of your responses - you can really start to take control of your life and create the life that you want for yourself. It all starts inside you and is not a consequence of what happens outside of you.

In this book, we have demonstrated that happiness and success are concepts which can be created, despite any plans the outside world might have for you. It is your inside world which dictates your life experience. Through the process outlined in this book, you have a simple and effective way to achieve the happy and fulfilling life you would like for yourself.

Following an exploration of the history of hypnosis, the mind and brain waves, we have gone on to show you the four levels of An Inside Job™ Self-Hypnosis. The greatest change will happen when you incorporate all four levels into your self-hypnosis practice. However, even if you only have time for the first level – breathing – you will bring about a greater sense of peace for yourself. As a refresher, the four levels are:

The First Level **Induction and Deepening**
Breathing and inducing self-hypnosis. This can be done on its own, to achieve a state of calm and grounding, or it can be used as a precursor to the other levels.

The Second Level **Affirmation**
Targeting yourself for success with goals. By focusing your mind on what you want, your behaviours start to form themselves around these goals so change is effected more easily.

The Third Level **Visualisation**
Incorporating visualisation into your self-hypnosis practice. What your mind can perceive you can achieve, as they say. It is like a dress-rehearsal for success.

The Fourth Level **Dealing with Inner Conflict**
This helps you to deal with any inner conflict you might be experiencing which stands in your way of achieving change. We are each made up of psychological parts which, for the most part, co-exist quite happily. However, sometimes they can be in conflict with each other, making change difficult. By exploring the positive intent of each part, it is possible to find a way forward to satisfy the needs of each part of your psyche, honouring your whole self.

Emerging Bringing yourself out of hypnosis when you have completed your practice.

Time for Yourself and Your Emotional Bank Account

It is important that loved ones respect your time and, by giving **yourself** this time, the quality of your time with **them** will be enhanced. You will have more to give because you will have given to yourself. As an example of this, if you have ever flown, you will be familiar with the safety announcements where you are instructed to put the oxygen mask on yourself prior to attending to anyone else. This is so that you are able to be more helpful to others in need. It is exactly the same when you take care of yourself. You might want to think of your self-hypnosis sessions in terms of "emotional hygiene". By regularly maintaining your emotional balance, you will have a greater bank of internal resources – uncluttered by emotional baggage - to be there for others. But you have to give to yourself first.

To be giving out all the time takes its toll on your emotional wellbeing and your health. This is an investment in yourself and also in your relationships.

Think of it as though you are making regular deposits in your emotional bank account. Before long you will have a whole fund from which you can draw from in difficult times, so that life's stressors can be negotiated far more easily. When there is an emotional recession on, others may struggle, but you will be fine because you have made sure you are through these regular deposits.

To get the best of your sessions, you need to prepare yourself well:

Preparation

To prepare yourself for self-hypnosis, all you have to do is find a nice comfortable place where you can relax. Preferably a place where you will not be disturbed. If this is difficult, instruct your family to leave you in peace for the amount of time you want to practice self-hypnosis.

Frequency and Duration

Regular practice is important. If you spring clean your house, it will be clean for a few days. But it won't be long before dust starts to gather, dishes will stack up in the sink, dirty laundry will be scattered over the floor and so on. If you clean a little every day, put dirty dishes in the dish washer and dirty laundry in the linen basket, you keep on top of things. Your weekly clean is easier and takes less time. If you spring clean after months of no housework, it is very difficult and it seems as though all you are doing is moving dust into the air only for it to settle back down on the surface again. In the same way, regular self-hypnosis is much better for you.

Spend a minimum of 5 minutes a day when you are only doing Level 1. When you start to increase the levels, it is better to spend 10-25 minutes. However, if time is short, even one minute is better than no time at all. But, like most things, the more you invest, the greater the return. Whatever the length of your session, it will include the induction and emerging elements.

Here is what a session might look like:

Level 1   Breathing and induction 3-5 minutes

Level 2   5-10 minutes

Level 3   3-5 minutes

Level 4   5 minutes or until the work is done

Emerge   Bringing yourself out of hypnosis when you have
            completed your practice

Of course, you can spend more time if you wish!

Benefits of An Inside ™ Self-Hypnosis ™

For a 10-25 minute investment of your time each day, these
are some of the benefits you can expect to enjoy from your
self-hypnosis practice:

- A greater sense of peace and calm
- Emotional resilience so that you bounce back
  from setbacks more easily
- Increased motivation for life in general and your
  goals in particular
- Improved self-esteem
- Emotional healing
- Positive change and neutralising any resistance to this
- Resolution of inner conflict
- Greater self-awareness
- More patience
- Greater physical wellbeing

Self-Hypnosis is Detoxifying

Because your self-hypnosis can be experienced as an emotional detox (depending on the kind of suggestions you choose), you may also find that you experience an emotional release (such as tears, or even anger). Whilst this will be quite rare, if you do, this is a sign that you are releasing suppressed emotions which need to come out. They are short term. You may also experience some physical symptoms such as a sore throat or rashes. Again, this is a function of the detox. Make sure you are drinking around 2 litres of water throughout the day and you will be supporting your body through this process. Very soon, the detoxing side of the practice will be done and you will only be experiencing the benefits.

Summary Tips

Set aside time

Set aside some time and tell people not to disturb you. Usually the same time each day makes it easier for the routine to become a natural part of your day.

My best time for self-hypnosis practice:

Intention

Set yourself an intention of how much time you will spend on your self-hypnosis practice – your subconscious mind is pretty good at keeping you to this. But it's OK for you to peek if you want to make sure you are on track. Whatever, you do, don't use an alarm clock as this can interfere with the subconscious process.

The amount of time I want to spend on my self-hypnosis practice:

Decide your goal

Decide what goal you want to achieve from the practice and which levels will support that.

My goal for hypnosis:

Select your suggestions

What suggestion(s) will support you? Some tips to help you:

- The present tense ie "I am" instead of "I will"
- Keep them short and simple
- Stated in the positive, (avoid "never", "don't", "won't" or "not"
- If you choose more than one, stay with one for several minutes before moving on to the next. Try and give all your suggestions an equal amount of time.

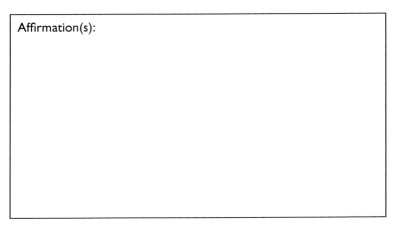

Make sure that you repeat the affirmation followed by the response each time. If you find yourself drifting off into a stream of thoughts, just bring yourself back to the affirmation:

Affirmation – response

Affirmation – response

Affirmation – response

Affirmation – response

Affirmation – response

Affirmation – response

And so on …

Repetition is essential in order to reprogram yourself.

Create your visualisation

What visualisation will work for you? Your visualisation is more powerful if you also think in terms of what you will hear and what you will feel.

```
Visualisation. What you will:

See:

Hear:

Feel:
```

Make sure the visualisation is powerful. Play around with the clarity, position and intensity of the picture, sounds and feelings. They need to be strong and compelling.

Identify conflicting parts

Consider whether there are any parts which are inhibiting your progress.

- The Inner Critic?
- The Pleaser?
- The Perfectionist?
- The Pusher?
- Other?

```
My Problematic Part:
```

Place in your least dominant hand and describe it:

- Colour
- Texture
- Shape
- Feeling
- Light or heavy
- Warm, hot or cold
- Soft or hard
- Any other defining features such as voice

What does that part need to balance itself?

- Nurturing Part?
- Confidence Part?
- Do it Now Part?
- Calm and Relaxed Part?
- Satisfied Part?
- Success Part?
- Other?

My Balancing Part:

Place this part into your dominant hand and describe it:

- Colour
- Texture
- Shape
- Feeling
- Light or heavy
- Warm, hot or cold
- Soft or hard
- Any other defining features

Once you have fully identified the parts and what they need:

1. Ask whether the parts are willing to work with each other

2. Negotiate any differences

3. Merge by turning the hands towards each other and, when you are ready, draw them towards your solar plexus and get the sense of them integrating with each other

Emerging

When you are done, emerge yourself from your self-hypnosis practice by counting backwards from 10-1. On the count of 1 you can open your eyes and notice how much calmer, more relaxed, and more resourceful you feel.

Drink water

As we mentioned earlier in the chapter, make sure you drink plenty of water during the day since self-hypnosis is a detoxing process and it will help support the physical aspects of this procedure.

A word about relaxation

You may or may not be relaxed during your self-hypnosis practice. Remember, hypnosis is not the same as relaxation. Every time will be a little different. A lot of the time you will not even **feel** hypnotised. The best thing is not to have any particular expectations and to simply know that it is working for you.

Frequency is better than duration

Daily practice is better for you than doing a big "blast" once a week. This not only builds momentum but also makes sure you don't get into any bad habits between sessions.

The more you practice, the quicker you will clear out any old baggage and start to create what you want for yourself.

About the CD

The CD is designed to aid your self-hypnosis practice and to guide you. Tricia and Helen's voices will be heard giving you a double-induction (where you will hear both of them at the same time) to deepen your hypnotic trance. You will then be given an opportunity to insert your own affirmations and visualisations and to undertake your parts therapy. There are three tracks:

1. Introduction

2. Hypnosis Track 1 which includes Levels 1, 2 and 3

3. Hypnosis Track 2 which includes Levels 1 and 4

The hypnosis tracks are around 25 minutes long. You can play them individually or consecutively if you have time.

As mentioned, you might want to listen to the tracks on your headphones to maximise the impact.

And Finally

We do hope you have enjoyed An Inside Job™. You now have simple, effective and enjoyable tools which will help you in life. Think of them as your most supportive friend. They are always there for you, whenever you need them. No matter what time of day or night. In good times and bad. Like any good friend, it makes the good times better and the bad times easier. It needs only one more ingredient – you! Change happens from the inside out – it's An Inside Job™ ! In truth it always was. You may not have known that before but you know that now. You don't need to be a victim of circumstances any more. You get to be the director of your life, to create and direct your own reality and An Inside Job™ is a huge part of that.

> *What you think about you bring about.*
> *Your whole life is a manifestation of the thoughts*
> *that go on in your head.*
>
> **Lisa Nichols**

9

NEXT STEPS AND RESOURCES

Helen and Tricia run self-hypnosis workshops to help you get even more from this experience. Learn from the creators in a supportive environment and share in their experience and expertise. Many people find that learning in such an environment is more powerful as the group energy takes the learning and spiritual aspects to a new level. It's a great opportunity, too, to ask all your burning questions and to reinforce your learning. To find out more, visit one of their websites below.

Websites:

www.thecravenclinic.co.uk

www.pw-hypnotherapy.co.uk

www.self-help-resources.co.uk

Books:

21 Ways and 21 Days to the Life You Want, Tricia Woolfrey

Think Positive, Feel Good, Tricia Woolfrey

Why Do I Do What I Do and Can I Change, Tricia Woolfrey (coming soon)

CDs/MP3

Relaxation, Helen Craven

Be Calm, Be Strong, Be Who You Really Are, Helen Craven

Sleep, Helen Craven

Find the Real You for Weight Loss, Helen Craven

Be Smoke-Free, Helen Craven

Relaxed and Confident for the Life You Want, Tricia Woolfrey

Ultimate Weight Loss, Tricia Woolfrey

Healthy Mind, Healthy Body, Tricia Woolfrey

Stop Smoking, Tricia Woolfrey

Controlling Anger by Tricia Woolfrey

Affirmations by Tricia Woolfrey

Wealth and Abundance by Tricia Woolfrey

Sleep Well by Tricia Woolfrey

Overcome ME by Tricia Woolfrey

Stress-Free by Tricia Woolfrey

E-Courses

ENERGISE – a system for energy enhancement by
Tricia Woolfrey

Anger – The Final Fronter. Understanding and
Conquering Anger, Tricia Woolfrey

10

ABOUT THE AUTHORS

Tricia Woolfrey is a highly experienced clinical hypnotherapist with a background in Human Resources, Training and Coaching. She has many years experience of helping people to realise their potential to get more from life, relationships and career. She offers therapy, coaching, training, health and stress coaching.

Tricia works in a wide variety of areas including self-confidence, anxiety, conflict management, depression, anger management, phobias, assertiveness, performance coaching, weight management and smoking cessation.

She has an HR consultancy (having previously been an HR Director) and a hypnotherapy practice in both Harley Street, London and Byfleet Village, Surrey and deals with groups and 1:1s.

She is qualified as an advanced clinical Hypnotherapist and Psychotherapist, and uses numerous techniques including CBT (Cognitive Behavioural Therapy), EFT (Emotional Freedom Technique), EMDR (Eye Movement Desensitisation Reprocessing) Theta Healing, Timeline, psychometric profiling, holistic nutrition, bioenergetics, food intolerance testing and The Balance Procedure.

She is a Fellow of the Chartered Institute of Personnel and Development, a member of the Association for Professional Hypnotherapists and Psychotherapists and a member of the General Hypnotherapy Register. She is a Master Practitioner with the National Centre for Eating Disorders and a Master Practitioner of Neuro Linguistic Programming.

The daughter of a French mother and a British father who was born and brought up in Morocco, Tricia too was born in Morocco, though she was brought up in the North of England from the age of one before moving to London in her mid-teens. She is the eldest of four, has a French half-sister, is happily married to Tom and has a dog, JJ. She lives in Surrey.

She runs numerous workshops for personal development, stress management, self-hypnosis and weight management, and has a range of CDs available, as well as inspirational products. For more information visit www.pw-hypnotherapy.co.uk and www.self-help-resources.co.uk.

She has appeared on BBC radio on numerous occasions and has appeared in several publications, both national and local.

If you have any questions or comments, please feel free to contact her at tricia@pw-hypnotherapy.co.uk.

Helen Craven has been working in the field of complementary therapies for over 20 years, the last half of which she has focused on clinical hypnotherapy. Having graduated top of her group from the Institute of Clinical Hypnosis, London, she has continued to undertake masterclasses and trainings with some of the best, cutting edge hypnosis trainers from around the world.

Areas of expertise include HypnoBirthing®, 5-PATH and 7th PATH, Ego States Therapy, Advanced Past Life Regression and Transpersonal Hypnosis, Life Between Lives Integration, The Balance Procedure, EFT (Emotional Freedom Technique). She is also a Reiki Master and Holistic Massage Therapist.

She has practices in Harley Street, London and Hythe, Kent.

She started life as an artist and designer and feels that was the start of her training, learning to look beneath the surface, to learn how things worked, question deeply to aid understanding and problem solve. Moving into therapy work was a seamless transfer of that, already well-developed, skill set. She moved from designing to writing, lecturing and curating exhibitions, gaining a Masters Degree from the Royal College of Art in Cultural History in 1987.

Three years later she agreed to temporarily run a friend's complementary health clinic as a favour. Always believing that "if you stop learning, you stop living", she embarked on a course of reading about, and experiencing, the different therapies and realised she had found a rewarding passion that overtook any other career path.

In 1997 she created The Craven Clinic in London W6, a multi-disciplinary health centre that brought together over 30 different therapies and also offered classes, courses and workshops.

From 2003 she decided to close the clinic in order to focus on her hypnotherapy work.

She is a member of the National Guild of Hypnotists.

www.thecravenclinic.co.uk

helencraven@talktalk.net